This Notebook Belongs To:

____

Made in the USA
Monee, IL
10 March 2021

62446780R00069